And round the throne, on each side of the throne,
are four living creatures . . . the first living creature like a lion,
the second living creature like an ox, the third living creature with
the face of a man, and the fourth living creature like a flying eagle.
And the four living creatures . . . day and night never cease to sing:
"Holy, holy, holy, is the Lord God Almighty,
Who was and is and is to come!"
—ADAPTED FROM REVELATIONS 4:6-8

LION: MARK
OX: LUKE
MAN: MATTHEW
EAGLE: JOHN

Jeanne Titherington

A Child's Prayer

Greenwillow Books
New York

Colored pencils were used for the full-color art.
The text type is ITC Isbell Book.

Library of Congress Cataloging-in-Publication Data

Titherington, Jeanne.   A child's prayer.
Summary: A little boy says his good-night
prayer before going to bed.
I. Children—Prayer-books and devotions—
English. [1. Prayers. 2. Christian life]
I. Title. BV265.T54
1989 242'.82 88-16566
ISBN 0-688-08317-x
ISBN 0-688-08318-8 (lib. bdg.)

To Anna,

a flower on the branch

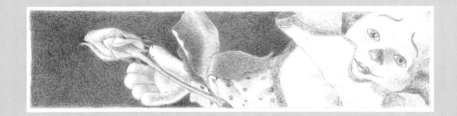

Matthew, Mark,
Luke, and John
bless the bed
that I lie on.

Before I lay me
down to sleep
I give myself
to God to keep.

Four corners to my bed,
four angels overspread:
One at the head,
one at the feet,
and two to guard me
while I sleep.

I go by sea,
I go by land,

The Lord made me
with His right hand.

If any danger
come to me,

O Blessed Lord,
deliver me.

He is the branch
and I'm the flower,

May God send me
a happy hour.